Tuning In

Peanuts can be read from beginning to end, but it may be more appropriate to read selected sections. Read pages 2–3 together as a group, using the teaching notes. Then share the contents sections between pairs of children and ask them to find out facts in their sections, recording as they do so. Support the children, with the help of the notes. Then finish the session by drawing the group back together and asking them what facts they have learnt.

The front cover

Look at the illustration. Have you ever eaten peanuts?

Do you like them?

What does it mean if someone says they are allergic to peanuts?

The back cover

Let's look at the back cover blurb. What does it tell us will be explained in this book?

Contents

Have you ever seen peanuts in their shells?

Which page will tell us about peanut farms?

How will the index help us?

READ

Read pages 2 and 3

Purpose: to identify different parts of the text, and find out how they help to explain what peanuts are, to find out why peanuts are so called.

EXPLORE

Pause at page 3

Which are the labels? What do they say?

Look at the photograph. Where does it show us that peanuts grow?

Why are 'peanuts' sometimes called 'groundnuts'? Who can find these words?

Were you surprised to find out that peanuts grow under the ground?

(Praise the children who understand how the caption relates to the illustration.)

What Are Peanuts?

Peanuts are the seeds
of the peanut plant.

They are called
peanuts because
they grow in
pods, like peas.
But the pods
are under the
ground.

That is why
peanuts are
sometimes called
groundnuts.

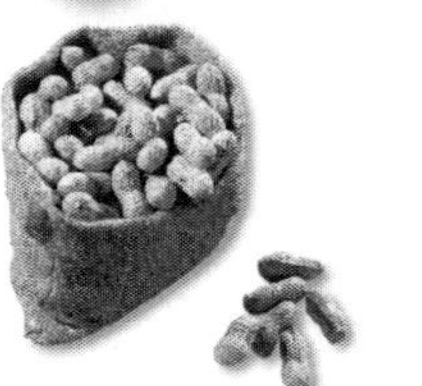

Read pages 4 and 5

Purpose: to understand the function of the map, and how to read the information it gives.

Pause at page 5

What does this map show?

What do the yellow areas on the map mean?

Find China on the map. Look at the small picture. What do you think the woman is doing in this picture?

Who can find Great Britain on the map? Do peanuts grow here? How can you tell?

Tricky words (page 5):
The words 'Thailand' and 'Australia' may be beyond the children's word recognition skills. Tell these words to the children.

Where Do Peanuts Grow?

Peanuts grow in warm parts of the world. Most of the world's peanuts are grown in these places:

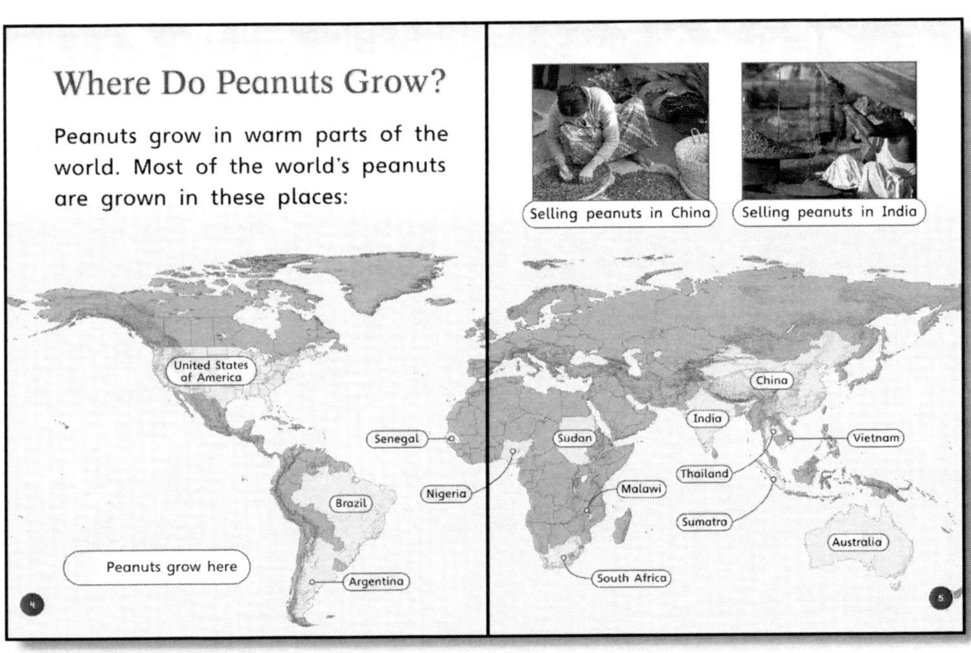

Selling peanuts in China

Selling peanuts in India

Read pages 6 and 7

Purpose: to find out how peanuts grow.

Pause at page 7

What does the title of these pages tell us we are going to find out about?

What does the illustration on page 7 show us?

Who can explain how peanut flowers are different from most other flowers?

How Do Peanuts Grow?

Peanut plants grow
yellow flowers on
long stems.

The flowers on most plants grow
towards the sun. But peanut
flowers grow down towards the
ground.

Then they grow into pods
with seeds in them.

READ

Read pages 8 and 9

Purpose: to find out what happens on peanut farms.

EXPLORE

Pause at page 9

How did you know what these pages were going to be about? *(heading)*

What is the difference between the peanuts in the hands and the peanuts growing under the ground? *(shells off)*

Read the text again on your own. Find out what happens after four or five weeks.

What happens to the pegs?

(Praise children who are reading fluently. If they are reading too slowly tell them to try and read the page as if they were talking.)

Peanut Farms

Peanut farmers
sow the seeds
in the soil.

The seeds are planted in rows, in
large fields.

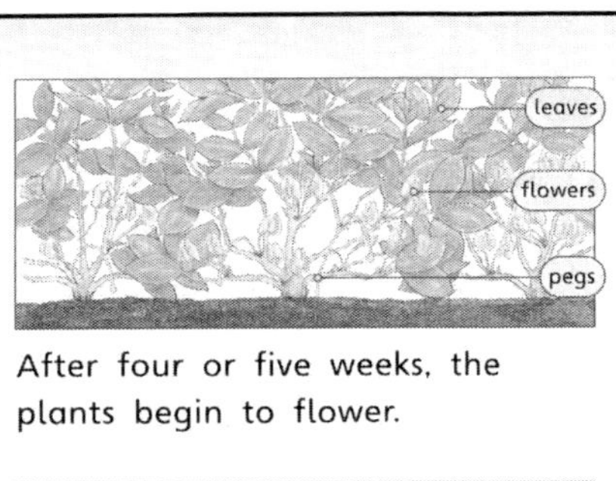

After four or five weeks, the
plants begin to flower.

Then the petals drop off, the pegs
go down into the soil and peanuts
begin to grow under the ground.

READ

Read pages 10 and 11

Purpose: to understand that this spread gives more information on how peanuts grow.

EXPLORE

Pause at page 11

Why do you think there isn't a heading on these pages? (*section continued from previous page*)

What is the farmer using to dig up the peanuts?

Read the text on your own and find out why the peanuts are left on the ground for a few days before being packed into sacks.

What do the captions tell us? (*what's happening in the photographs*)

When the peanuts are ready, the
farmer digs them up.

The peanuts are left to dry in
the sun for a few days. Then
they are packed into sacks.

Read pages 12 and 13

Purpose: to read a simple flow diagram.

Pause at page 13

What do you think the arrows mean?

What do you notice about the shape of the illustrations?

What happens to peanuts when they reach the factory?

(Praise children who can read the verbs 'shelled', 'cleaned', 'roasted'.)

Peanut Factories

The sacks of peanuts are sent
to factories all over the world.

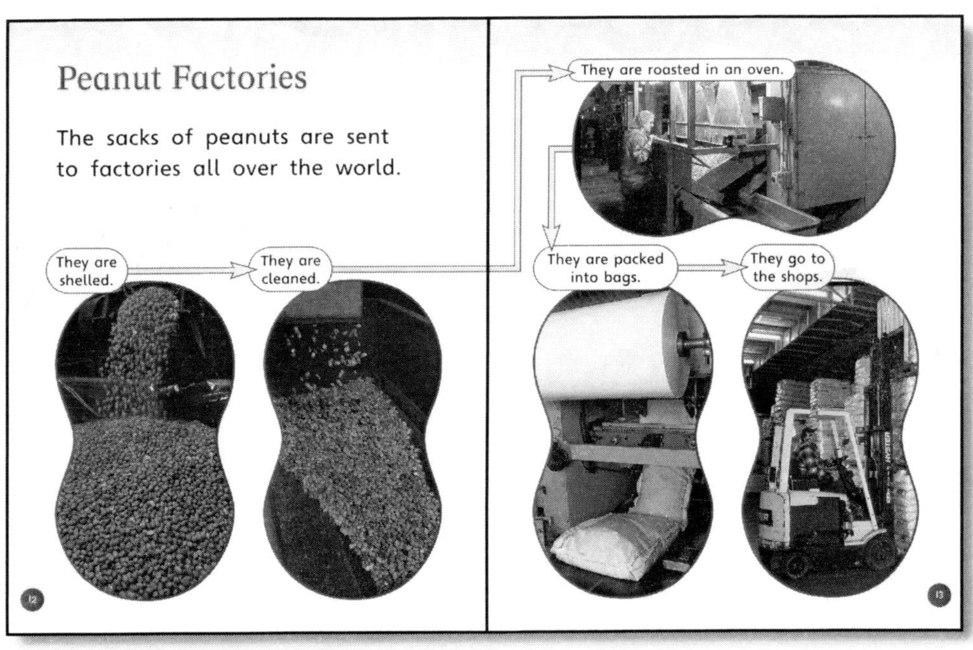

READ

Read pages 14 and 15

Purpose: to notice how the information in these pages is different from the rest of the book.

EXPLORE

Pause at page 15

What is different in these pages from the previous pages? *(drawings, cartoons, not photographs)*

What are all the children doing in these drawings?

Look at the warning in the box. What do you think allergic means?

How do you like to eat peanuts?

READ

Read page 16

Purpose: to use the index to find information.

EXPLORE

Pause at page 16

Do story books have an index?

Why do you think this book has two page numbers beside 'factories' and 'shelled peanuts'?

Which pages tell us about the peanut flowers?

Tricky words (page 15):
The word 'sauce' may be beyond the children's word recognition skills. Tell this word to the children.

The word 'allergic' may also want to be discussed as a tricky word.

Eating Peanuts

Peanuts can be eaten in many different ways!

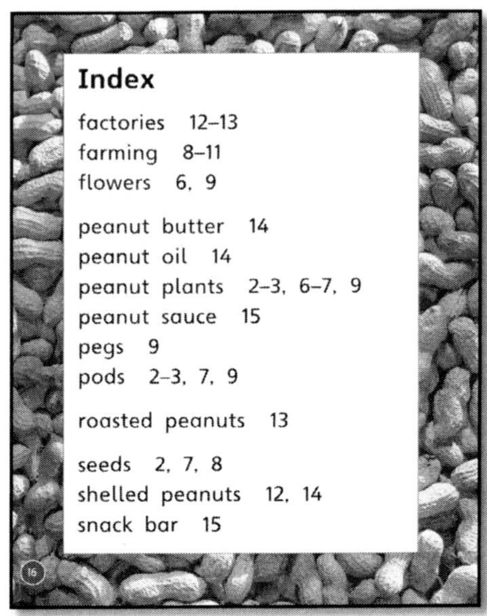

Index

After Reading
Revisit and Respond

- Peanuts is an explanation text. What does it explain? Why are peanuts called 'peanuts'?

- What three facts did you learn in this book that you did not know before?

- How would you find out about peanut farms without reading the whole book?

- Look through the headings in this book. Find the ones that ask a question. What punctuation do you need to put at the end of a question?

- Find 'shelled', 'cleaned', 'roasted', 'packed', on page 13, e.g like 'ed' in 'cleaned' but like 't' in 'packed'.